MESHUGGAH FOOD FACES

by Bill and Claire Wurtzel

BEHRMAN HOUSE
www.behrmanhouse.com

Meshuggah Food Faces is dedicated to our parents. They nourished us with love, food, playfulness, and Yiddishkeit. We hope our rye sense of Jewish humor brings some joy to this meshuggah world. May these dishes give you belly laughs, not heartburn. —Bill and Claire

We wish to thank Ann Koffsky, Dena Neusner, and Susan & David Neuhaus, whose talent and vision helped shape this book. Also, thanks to Behrman House for being meshuggah enough to take us on.

Published by Behrman House, Inc.
Millburn, New Jersey 07041
www.behrmanhouse.com

ISBN 978-1-68115-066-6
Copyright © 2020 by William Wurtzel and Claire Wurtzel

Library of Congress Cataloging-in-Publication Data
Names: Wurtzel, Bill, author. | Wurtzel, Claire, author.
Title: Meshuggah food faces / by Bill and Claire Wurtzel.
Description: Millburn, New Jersey : Behrman House, [2020] | Summary: "Foods with feelings have photo funny faces"— Provided by publisher.
Identifiers: LCCN 2020019026 | ISBN 9781681150666 (hardcover)
Subjects: LCSH: Jewish wit and humor. | Food presentation—Humor.
Classification: LCC PN6231.J5 W87 2020 | DDC 818/.5402—dc23
LC record available at https://lccn.loc.gov/2020019026

Design by Susan and David Neuhaus/NeuStudio
Edited by Ann D. Koffsky

Printed in the United States of America

1 3 5 7 9 8 6 4 2

How are you?

How should I be?

Happiness is a bowl of chicken soup.

Get off your tush and work out.

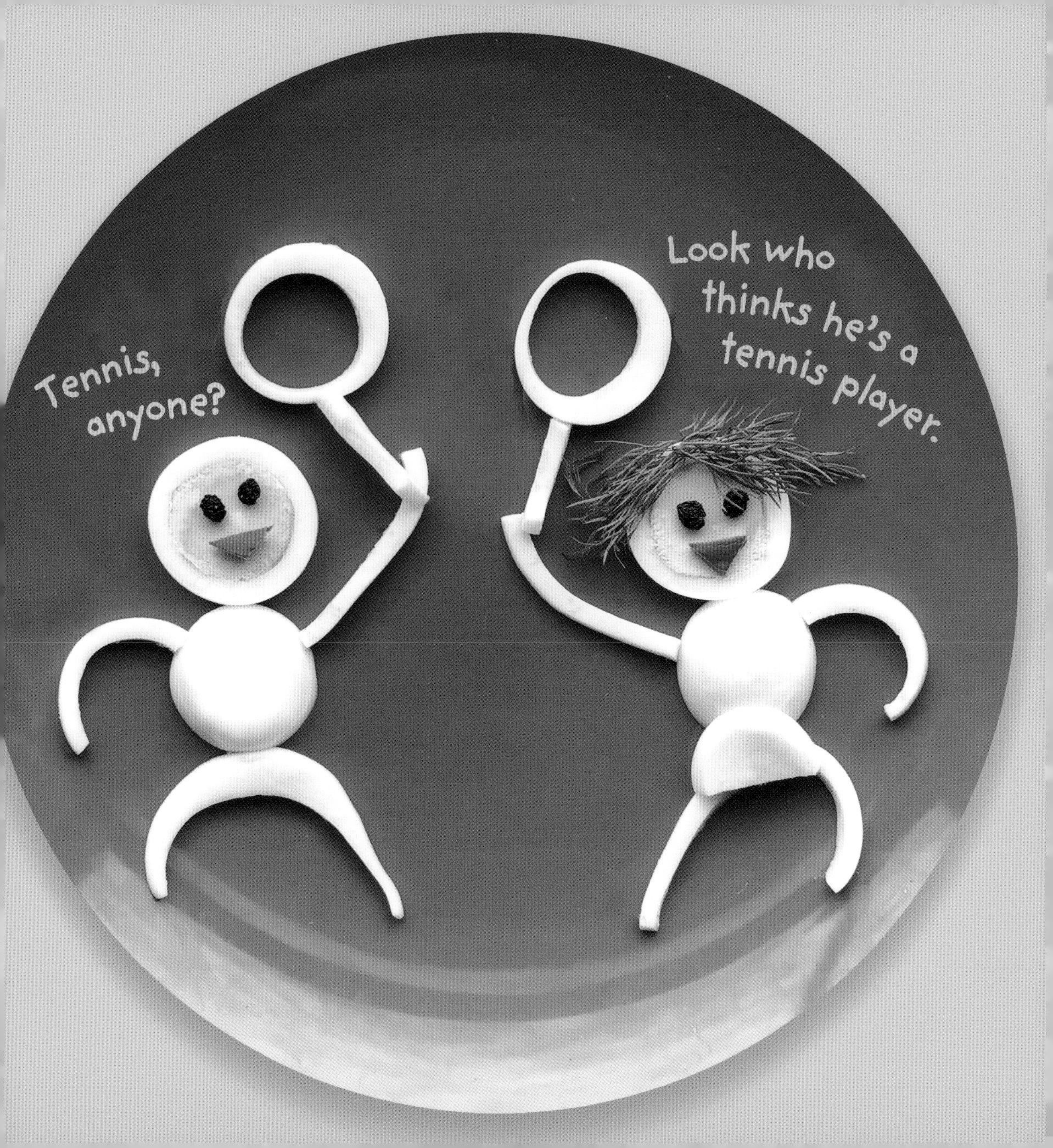
Tennis, anyone?
Look who thinks he's a tennis player.

It's fun to be a fashion plate.

Oy, am I blue!

If life doesn't change for the better, wait...

... and it will change for the worse.

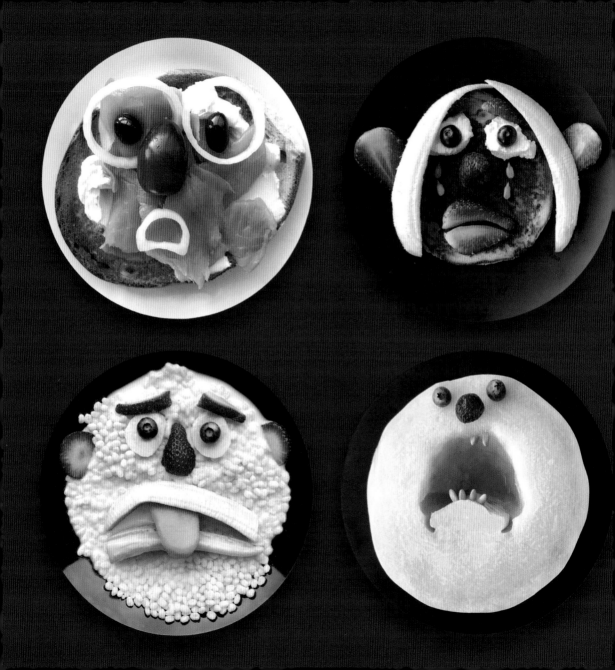

Now THIS is a bad hair day.

WHAT,
ME STRESSED?

Some days
I feel like
Flankenstein.

the strangest places.

Famous friendly faces

Pinestein

R. B. Greensburg

Banana Streisand

Sigmund Fruit

Blintz buddies

You're
everything

friend is cracked
up to be.

Does your *mishpachah**
make you *meshuggah?*

*family

Look how he holds the balloon.

He's a regular genius.

Bubbe and Zaide

Cousin Yetta the Yenta

Flaky Aunt Flo

Uncle Max the Macher

I love you,
Poppy.

Is this is a *shidduch** or what?

*perfect match

Look what can
happen with a
couple of dates.

Novie

Seeks other half with the whole schmear.

Tabouli

Seeks a match who doesn't mind Moroccan cigars.

Mel

Seeks partner who's also a bigmouth.

Stache

Seeks woman who'll be tickled by a mustache.

Piney

Pining away, hoping to meet a perfect match.

Porridgeo

Seeks fun-loving, oatgoing cereal lover.

Rugelach
Confectionate
sweetie seeks
smart cookie.

Omeletta
Seeks good
egg who
keeps their
sunny side up.

Yogurtrude
Seeks fat-free
partner who is
a good mixer.

Wafflina
Seeks mate
who won't
waffle about
marriage.

Veggie
Seeks partner
with lots of
cabbage.

Tutti-Fruity
Seeks berry
fruitful
relationship.

I'm out on my own . . . hot dog!

All dressed up for the challahdays!

Put on your
holiday face.

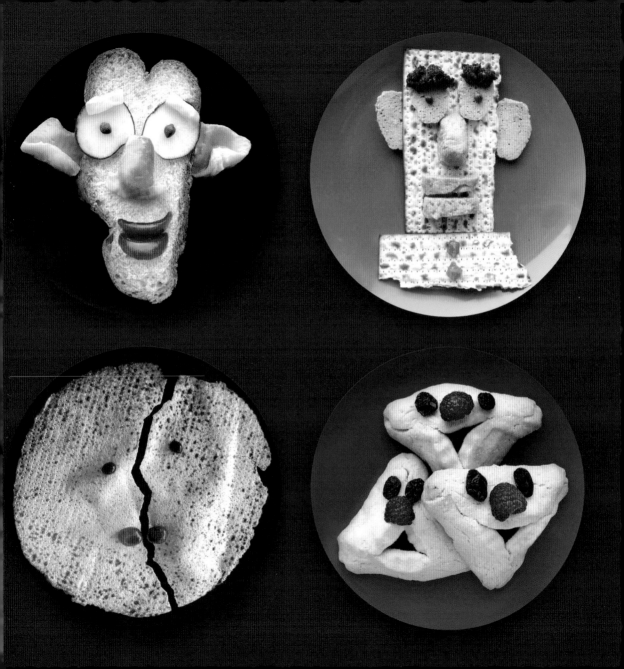

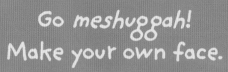

Go *meshuggah!*
Make your own face.

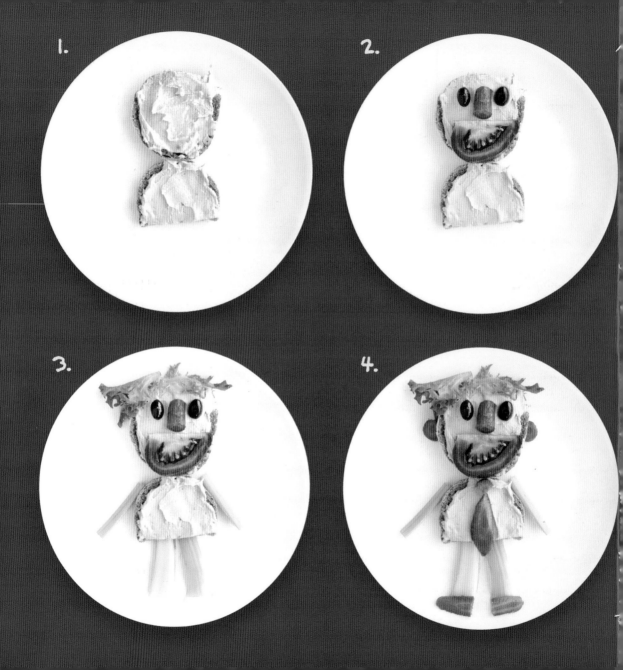

1.

2.

3.

4.

1.

2.

3.

4.

Bill Wurtzel is an artist and jazz musician, so improvisation, even with food, comes naturally to him. In his previous career as an advertising creative director, he won over 200 awards. Bill began making food art to amuse his wife, Claire, when they were married in 1961. Today, Bill and Claire conduct workshops using his food art to make it fun for children and families to learn about nutrition.

Claire Wurtzel is an educator. She was a professor at the Bank Street College of Education and is currently the co-educational director of Hidden Sparks. When Claire was a child, her mother made challah and shaped the extra dough into funny objects like little birds or feet with cinnamon and raisins to look like dirt between the toes. Bill is carrying on the tradition.

Bill and Claire have collaborated on *Funny Food* and three other books of food art.